Preface 序

Mandarin Chinese is the second most prolific language in the world, but many people will think it is one of the most difficult languages to learn, especially due to its characters and tones.

This series of textbooks introduces the concept that knowing 100 basic Chinese characters can help learners to conquer these learning difficulties. Even though there are about 3000 frequently used characters, children need only learn 100 basic characters at first. After which the E-Pen software accompanying this series of textbooks can be used to assist children in typing on the computer. In this way, learning Chinese will not be so hard anymore.

In addition, traditional characters have been in use longer than the simplified characters and for this reason often shows much more of the Chinese cultural heritage. We suggest that young learners learn the traditional characters in the beginning to establish a good basis. This series of textbooks – K1 and K2 teach 33 traditional characters, which are all the same with the simplified characters, and K3 provides both traditional and simplified characters.

華語是全球第二大語言，但是許多人認為華語是最難學的外語之一，因為「漢字如天書」。本教材提出 100 基本漢字的觀念，試圖打破華語是難學外語的刻板印象。常用漢字有 3000 字，但只要學會約 100 個基本漢字，未來再配合 E-Pen（電腦筆）軟體，漢字就不難了。本教材 K1 與 K2 所學習的 33 個字全都是正簡相同的漢字，K3 則正體字並列簡化字。

生活華語 第 K1 冊

Helping Tips for Teachers and Parents

Preface

1 Tones 3

2 Numbers 6

3 Please 10

4 人 People/Man 16

5 大 Big 18

6 小 Little/Small 20

7 口 Mouth 24

8 日 Sun/Day 26

9 月 Moon/Month 28

10 早 Morning 32

11 山 Mountain 34

12 木 Wood 36

For teachers and parents **Song & Game**

妈 妈
媽ㄇㄚ 媽˙ㄇㄚ 早ㄗㄠˇ！爸ㄅㄚˋ 爸˙ㄅㄚ 早ㄗㄠˇ！ *Good morning, Mom!*
mā   ma   zǎo   bà   ba   zǎo   *Good morning, Dad!*

来 亲 亲 来
來ㄌㄞˊ 親ㄑㄧㄣ 親ㄑㄧㄣ，來ㄌㄞˊ 抱ㄅㄠˋ 抱˙ㄅㄠ。 *Come give me a kiss!*
lái   qīn   qīn   lái   bào   bào   *Come give me a hug!*
      cīn   cīn

4 Tones: Let's practice the 4 tones.

mā	má	mǎ	mà
(mom)	(numb)	(horse)	(scolding)

請聽老師唸，並貼上貼紙。Listen and place the stickers.

Tones	1st tone —	2nd tone ╱	3rd tone ∨	4th tone ╲
mā				
má				
mǎ				
mà				

❶ 老ㄌㄠˇ師ㄕ好ㄏㄠˇ！小ㄒㄧㄠˇ朋ㄆㄥˊ友ㄧㄡˇ好ㄏㄠˇ！ *Hello, teacher!*
   lǎo shī hǎo　　xiǎo péng yǒu hǎo *Hello, children!*
   　　 shīh　　　siǎo

❷ 媽ㄇㄚ媽ㄇㄚ早ㄗㄠˇ！爸ㄅㄚˋ爸ㄅㄚ早ㄗㄠˇ！ *Good morning, Mom!*
   mā ma zǎo　　bà ba zǎo *Good morning, Dad!*

課室活動：使用「爸爸、媽媽、老師、小朋友」四張圖卡進行角色扮演。

2 Numbers

For teachers and parents **Song & Game**

一 — 二 ㄦ 三 ㄙㄢ 拍 ㄆㄞ 拍 ㄆㄞ 手 ㄕㄡ 。 *One, two, three, clap (your) hands.*
yī èr sān pāi pāi shǒu

点 点 头
四 ㄙ 五 ㄨ 六 ㄌㄡ 點 ㄉㄢ 點 ㄉㄢ 頭 ㄊㄡ 。 *Four, five, six, nod (your) head.*
sì wǔ liù diǎn diǎn tóu
sìh   liòu

来
七 ㄑㄧ 八 ㄅㄚ 九 ㄐㄧㄡ 來 ㄌㄞ 洗 ㄒㄧ 手 ㄕㄡ 。 *Seven, eight, nine, come wash (your) hands.*
qī bā jiǔ lái xǐ shǒu
cī   jiǒu   sǐ

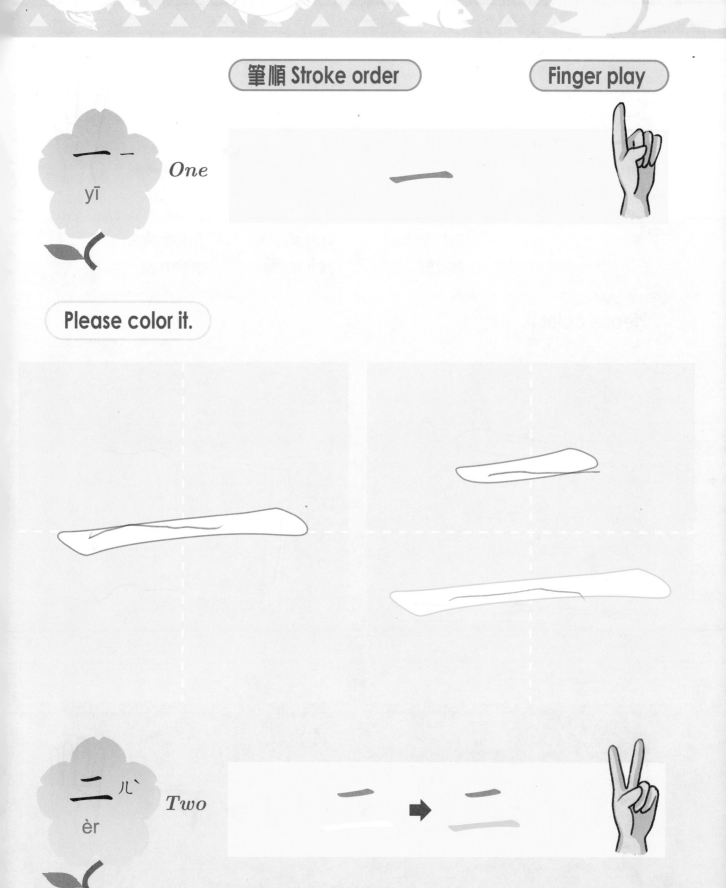

筆順 Stroke order

Finger play

One

yī

Please color it.

二 ㄦ Two

èr

 *Three*

| 1st stroke red 紅 | → | 2nd stroke yellow 黃 | → | 3rd stroke green 綠 |

Please color it.

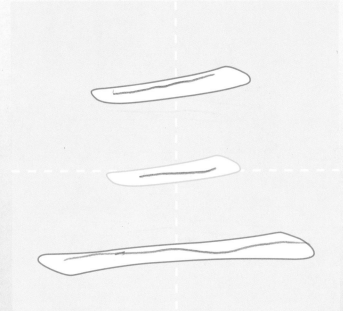

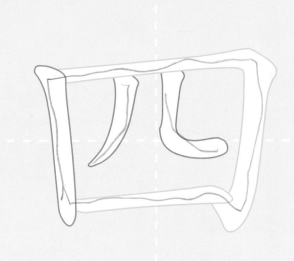

 四 ㄙ
sì
sìh   *Four*

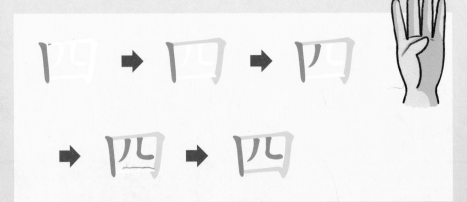

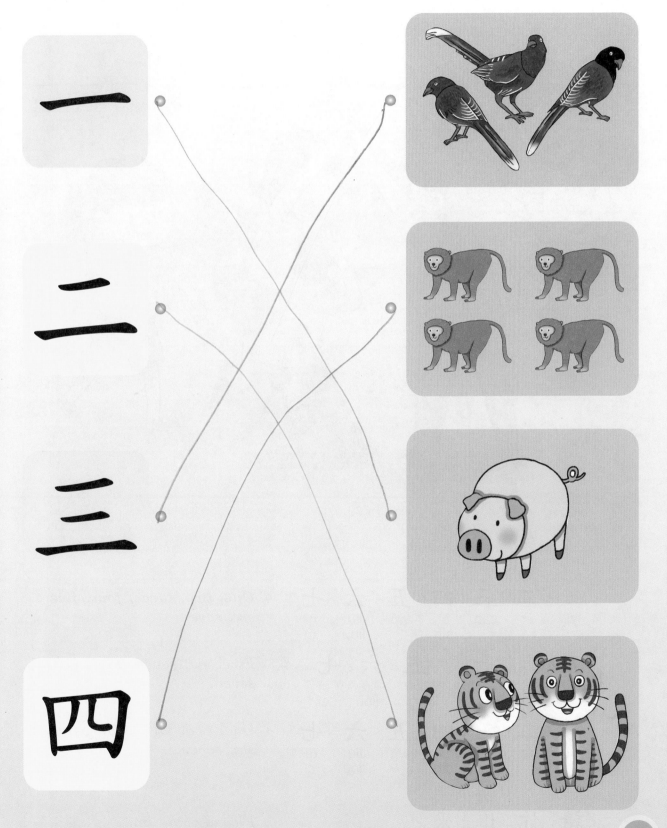

一

二

三

四

數一數　連連看　Count and match

一 二 三 四 五 六 七 。
yī èr sān sì wǔ liù qī
          sìh   liòu cī

One, two, three, four, five, six, seven.

五 六 七 ， 五 六 七 。
wǔ liù qī   wǔ liù qī
   liòu cī   liòu cī

Five, six, seven. Five, six, seven.

一 二 三 四 五 六 七 ，
yī èr sān sì wǔ liù qī
          sìh   liòu cī

One, two, three, four, five, six, seven.

请 进 来
請 你 進 來 。
qǐng nǐ jìn lái
cǐng

Please come in.

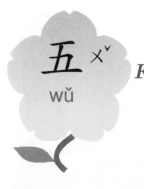

五　ㄨˇ　*Five*
wǔ

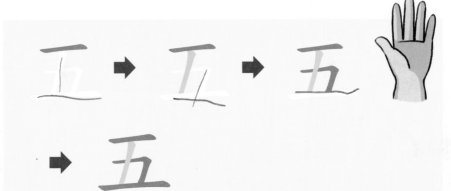

Please color it.

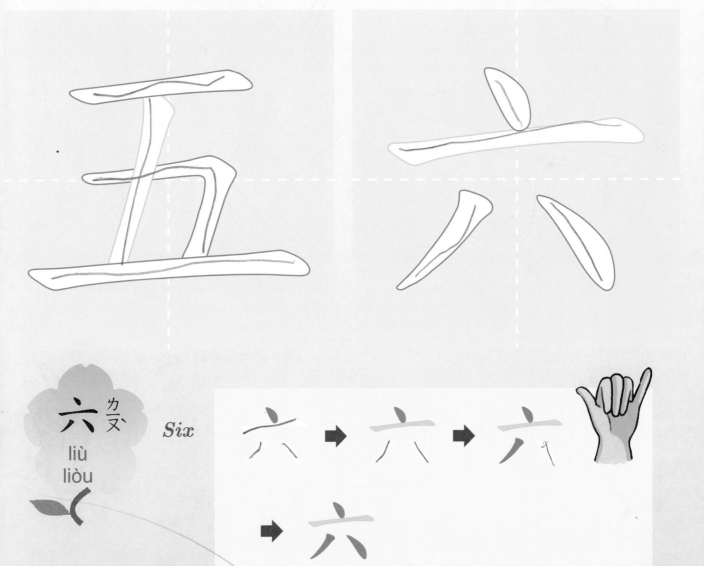

六　ㄌㄧㄡˋ　*Six*
liù
liòu

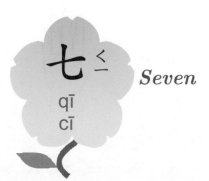
七
くー
qī
cī

Seven

七 ➡ 七

Please color it.

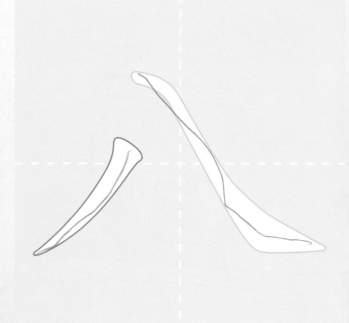

八
クY
bā

Eight

八 ➡ 八

九 ㄐㄧㄡˇ
jiǔ
jiǒu

Nine

九 ➡ 九

Please color it.

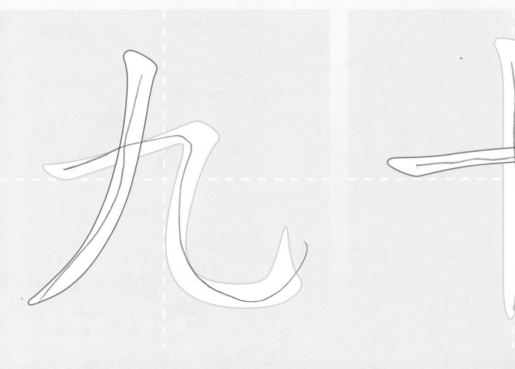

十 ㄕˊ
shí
shíh

Ten

一 ➡ 十

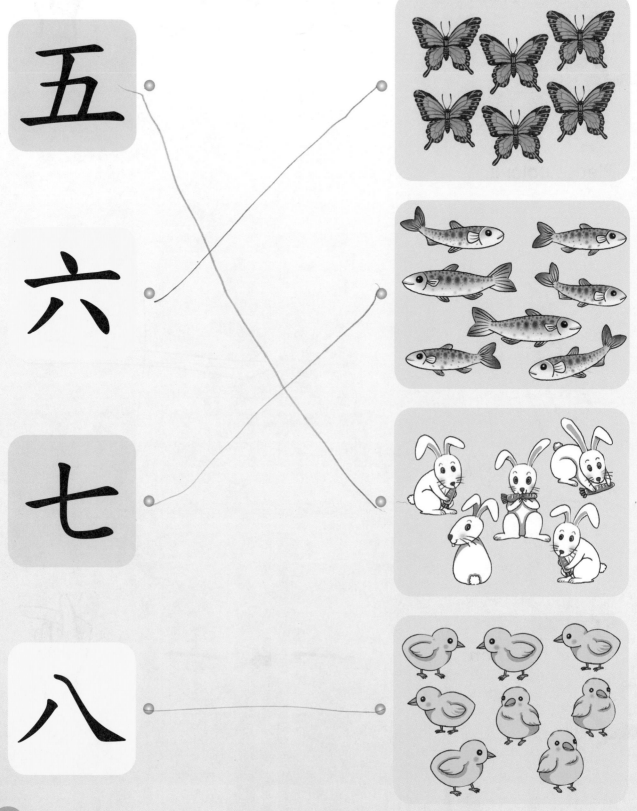

請聽老師唸，並貼上貼紙。Listen and place the stickers.

Tones	1ˢᵗ tone —	2ⁿᵈ tone ╱	3ʳᵈ tone ∨	4ᵗʰ tone ╲
一				
二				
三				
四				
五				

人 rén *People/Man*

一 一 二 儿 三 ㄙㄢ ， 木 ㄇㄨ 頭 ㄊㄡ 人 ㄖㄣ 。 *One, two, three. Wood Man.*
yī   èr   sān   mù   tóu   rén

不 ㄅㄨ 要 一ㄠ 跑 ㄆㄠ ！ 不 ㄅㄨ 要 一ㄠ 動 ㄉㄨㄥ ！ *Don't run! Don't move!*
bú   yào   pǎo   bú   yào   dòng

人 ▶ 人

Please color it.

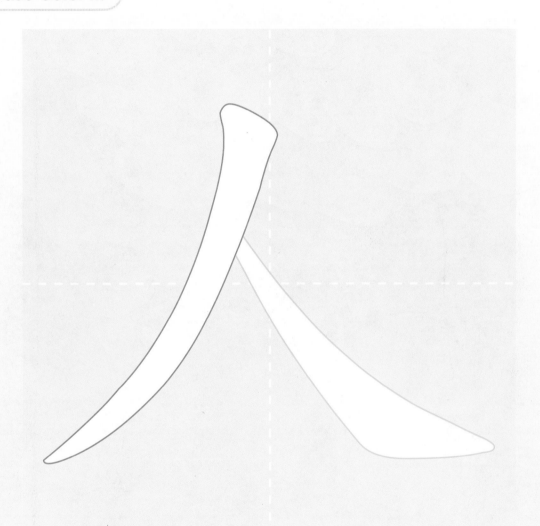

① 不ㄅㄨˊ要ㄧㄠˋ插ㄔㄚ隊ㄉㄨㄟˋ！不ㄅㄨˊ要ㄧㄠˋ爭ㄓㄥ吵ㄔㄠˇ！
　　bú　yào　chā　duì　　　bú　yào　zhēng　chǎo
　　　　　　　　　　　队／duèi　　　　　　　争／jhēng

Don't cut in!
Don't fight!

② 我ㄨㄛˇ要ㄧㄠˋ筆ㄅㄧˇ。我ㄨㄛˇ要ㄧㄠˋ紙ㄓˇ。
　　wǒ　yào　bǐ　　　wǒ　yào　zhǐ
　　　　　　笔　　　　　　　　纸／jhǐh

I want a pen.
I want paper.

課室活動：老師說：「不要跑」，學生做跳的動作。
　　　　　老師說：「不要跳」，學生做跑的動作。

17

大 ㄉㄚ dà *Big/Huge*

大熊ㄒㄩㄥ 大ㄉㄚ，大ㄉㄚ 熊ㄒㄩㄥ 大ㄉㄚ，大ㄉㄚ 熊ㄒㄩㄥ 愛ㄞ 爬ㄆㄚ 樹ㄕㄨ，
dà xióng dà，dà xióng dà，dà xióng ài pá shù
syóng syóng syóng

天ㄊㄢ 天ㄊㄢ 笑ㄒㄧㄠ 哈ㄏㄚ 哈ㄏㄚ！
tiān tiān xiào hā hā
siào

Big bears are big, Big bears love to climb trees and laugh everyday. Ha! Ha! Ha!

Please color it.

① 課室活動：兩人一組，玩猜拳，贏的人說：「我愛你」，
輸的人說：「來抱抱」，兩人相互抱在一起。

② 課室活動：第一個小朋友說：「我愛吃梨子」。
第二個小朋友說：「你愛吃梨子，我愛吃蛋糕。」

6　小 xiǎo / siǎo *Little/Small*

小 ← 小 ← 小 ← ⋯

大朋友小朋友，點點頭握握手。
dà péng yǒu xiǎo péng yǒu diǎn diǎn tóu wò wò shǒu
siǎo

你三歲我四歲，我們都是好朋友。
nǐ sān suì wǒ sì suì wǒ men dōu shì hǎo péng yǒu
suèi sìh suèi shìh

20 *Big friends, little friends. Nodding heads and shaking hands.*
You are three (and) I am four. We are all good friends.

小 ➡ 小 ➡ 小

Please color it.

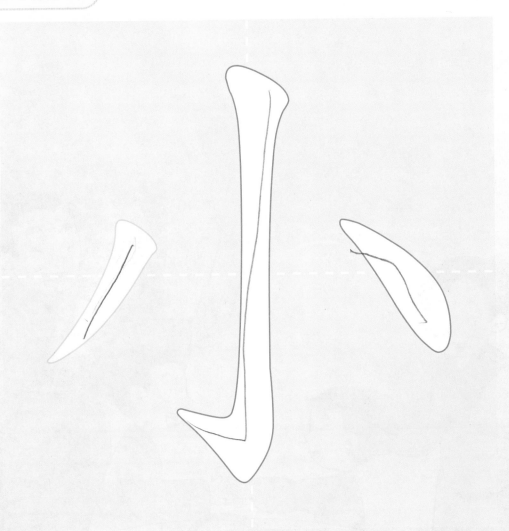

① 你ㄋˇㄧ 幾ㄐˇㄧ 歲ㄙㄨㄟˋ？　　　我ㄨㄛˇ 三ㄙㄢ 歲ㄙㄨㄟˋ。
　　nǐ　jǐ　suì　　　　　wǒ　sān　suì
　　　　　　suèi　　　　　　　　　suèi

How old are you?　　　*I am three years old.*

② 課室活動：小朋友排成兩列，面對面互做點頭握手的動作後，
　　　　　　　交互詢問對方「你幾歲？」。完成後，往右移動，
　　　　　　　再重複以上活動。

21

小 ← 🍐　　大 ← 🍐

（文化故事：孔融讓梨）

請聽老師唸，並貼上貼紙。Listen and place the stickers.

Tones	1st tone —	2nd tone ╱	3rd tone ∨	4th tone ╲
人				
大				
小				
六				
七				

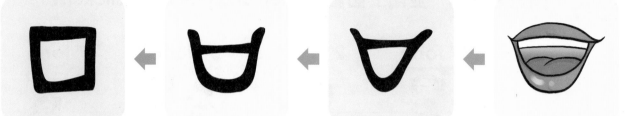

小ㄒㄧㄠˇ白ㄅㄞˊ鵝ㄜˊ，ge-ge-ge，口ㄎㄡˇ渴ㄎㄜˇ了ㄌㄜ，叫ㄐㄧㄠˋ哥ㄍㄜ哥ㄍㄜ。
xiǎo bái é   kǒu kě le   jiào gē ge
siǎo

肚ㄉㄨˋ子ㄗ餓ㄜˋ，叫ㄐㄧㄠˋ哥ㄍㄜ哥ㄍㄜ，ge-ge-ge，ge-ge-ge。
dù zi è   jiào gē ge
   zih

Little geese, ge-ge-ge. Get thirsty, call elder brother (Ge-Ge).
Get hungry, call elder brother (Ge-Ge).

日 ➡ 日 ➡ 日 ➡ 日

Please color it.

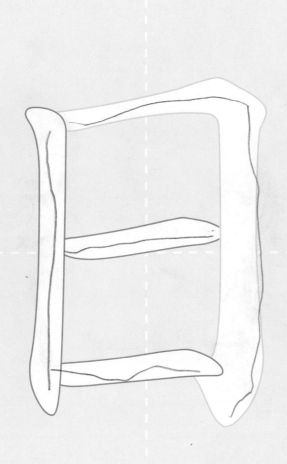

① 祝^{ㄓㄨ}你^{ㄋㄧ}新^{ㄒㄧㄣ}年^{ㄋㄧㄢ}快^{ㄎㄨㄞ}樂^{乐
ㄌㄜ}！ *Happy New Year (to you)!*
　zhù　nǐ　xīn　nián　kuài　lè
　jhù　　　sīn

② 謝^{谢
ㄒㄧㄝ}謝^{谢
ㄒㄧㄝ}。　*Thanks.*
　xiè　xie
　siè　sie

課室活動：教唱生日快樂歌

27

月ㄩㄝ 兒ㄦ 彎ㄨㄢ 弯 ， 月ㄩㄝ 兒ㄦ 亮ㄌㄤ ， *The moon is curved.*
yuè ēr wān yuè ēr liàng *The moon is bright.*

月ㄩㄝ 兒ㄦ 彎ㄨㄢ 彎ㄨㄢ 弯 弯 真ㄓㄣ 漂ㄆㄠ 亮ㄌㄤ 。 *The curved moon is so pretty.*
yuè ēr wān wān zhēn piào liàng
jhēn

月 ➡ 月 ➡ 月 ➡ 月

Please color it.

① 這是月亮嗎？是／不是。 Is this the moon?
　　这　　　　吗　　　　　　　　　　　　　Yes, it is. / No, it is not.
　　zhè shì yuè liàng ma　shì　bú shì
　　jhè shìh　　　　　　　shìh　　shìh

② 這是大熊嗎？是／不是。 Is this a big bear?
　　这　　　　吗　　　对　　　　对　　　Yes, it is. / No, it is not.
　　zhè shì dà xióng ma　shì　bú shì
　　jhè shìh　　syóng　　shìh　　shìh

課室活動：看圖練習「是／不是」的問答活動。

29

 請聽老師唸，並貼上貼紙。Listen and place the stickers.

月 ← 日 ←

Maze of "月"

開始
Start

（文化故事：嫦娥奔月）

請聽老師唸，並貼上貼紙。Listen and place the stickers.

Tones	1st tone ―	2nd tone ／	3rd tone ∨	4th tone ＼
口				
日				
月				
八				
九				

31

早 ㄗㄠˇ zǎo *Morning*

早 ← 早 ← 早 ←

（圖中的草在古書裡為盔甲圖）

刷ㄕㄨㄚ 刷ㄕㄨㄚ 牙ㄧㄚˊ ，漱ㄕㄨˋ 漱ㄕㄨˋ 口ㄎㄡˇ ，
shuā shuā yá shù shù kǒu

Brush (your) teeth.
Rinse (your) mouth.

早ㄗㄠˇ 睡ㄕㄨㄟˋ 早ㄗㄠˇ 起ㄑㄧˇ 身ㄕㄣ 體ㄊㄧˇ 好ㄏㄠˇ 。
zǎo shuì zǎo qǐ shēn tǐ hǎo
shuèi cǐ
体

Early to bed early to rise keeps (your) body healthy.

早 ➔ 早 ➔ 早 ➔ 早 ➔ 早 ➔ 早

Please color it.

1. 你ㄋㄧˇ 刷ㄕㄨㄚ 牙ㄧㄚˊ 了ㄌㄜ 吗/嗎ㄇㄚ？ 我ㄨㄛˇ 刷ㄕㄨㄚ 牙ㄧㄚˊ 了ㄌㄜ。 *Did you brush (your) teeth? I brushed (my) teeth.*
   nǐ   shuā   yá   le   ma   wǒ   shuā   yá   le

2. 刷ㄕㄨㄚ 牙ㄧㄚˊ ➔ 刷ㄕㄨㄚ 刷ㄕㄨㄚ 牙ㄧㄚˊ *Brush teeth*   漱ㄕㄨˋ 口ㄎㄡˇ ➔ 漱ㄕㄨˋ 漱ㄕㄨˋ 口ㄎㄡˇ *Rinse mouth*
   shuā   yá   shuā   shuā   yá   shù   kǒu   shù   shù   kǒu

   点/點ㄉㄧㄢˇ 头/頭ㄊㄡˊ ➔ 早 *Nod head*   握ㄨㄛˋ 手ㄕㄡˇ ➔ 早 *Shake hands*
   diǎn   tóu   wò   shǒu

33

11 山 ㄕㄢ shān *Mountain*

一一二ㄦ三ㄙ四ㄙ五ㄨ，山ㄕㄢ上ㄕㄤ有ㄧㄡ老ㄌㄠ虎ㄏㄨ。
yī èr sān sì wǔ shān shàng yǒu lǎo hǔ
sìh

几只
老ㄌㄠ虎ㄏㄨ有ㄧㄡ幾ㄐ隻ㄓ？一一二ㄦ三ㄙ四ㄙ五ㄨ。
lǎo hǔ yǒu jǐ zhī yī èr sān sì wǔ
jhīh sìh

(34) *One, two, three, four, five. There are tigers in the mountain.*
How many tigers? One, two, three, four, five.

山 ➔ 山 ➔ 山

Please color it.

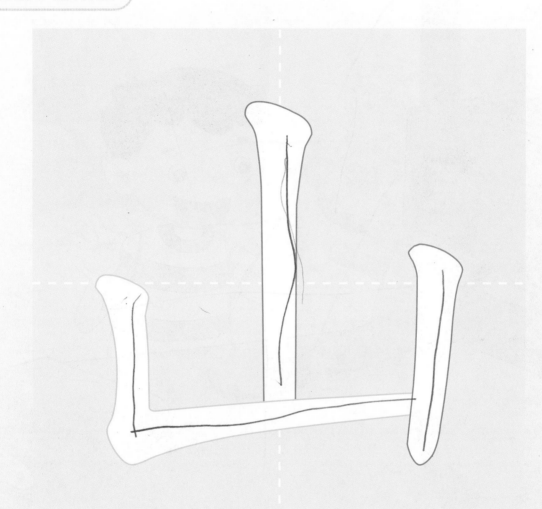

① 山ㄕㄢ上ㄕㄤ有ㄧㄡˇ老ㄌㄠˇ虎ㄏㄨˇ嗎ㄇㄚ˙？有ㄧㄡˇ／没ㄇㄟˊ有ㄧㄡˇ。
shān shàng yǒu lǎo hǔ ma yǒu méi yǒu

② 你ㄋㄧˇ有ㄧㄡˇ筆ㄅㄧˇ嗎ㄇㄚ˙？我ㄨㄛˇ有ㄧㄡˇ／我ㄨㄛˇ没ㄇㄟˊ有ㄧㄡˇ。
nǐ yǒu bǐ ma wǒ yǒu wǒ méi yǒu

Are there tigers in the mountain? Yes, there are. / No, there are not.
Do you have a pen? Yes, I do. / No, I don't.

課室活動：看圖練習「有／没有」的問答活動。

木 ㄇㄨˋ　*mù*　*Wood*

小ㄒㄧㄠˇ 木ㄇㄨˋ 偶ㄡˇ， 小ㄒㄧㄠˇ 木ㄇㄨˋ 偶ㄡˇ， 請ㄑㄧㄥˇ 你ㄋㄧˇ 彎ㄨㄢ 彎ㄨㄢ 腰ㄧㄠ，
xiǎo mù ǒu　xiǎo mù ǒu　qǐng nǐ wān wān yāo
siǎo　　　　siǎo　　　　cǐng

請ㄑㄧㄥˇ 你ㄋㄧˇ 揮ㄏㄨㄟ 揮ㄏㄨㄟ 手ㄕㄡˇ， 你ㄋㄧˇ 是ㄕˋ 我ㄨㄛˇ 的ㄉㄜ 好ㄏㄠˇ 朋ㄆㄥˊ 友ㄧㄡˇ。
qǐng nǐ huī huī shǒu　nǐ shì wǒ de hǎo péng yǒu
cǐng　　huēi huēi　　　　shìh

Little puppet, Little puppet, please bend down,
Please wave your hands.　You are my good friend.

木 ➡ 木 ➡ 木 ➡ 木

Please color it.

① 他ㄊㄚ 是ㄕˋ shì 誰ㄕㄟˊ shéi shíh ?　他ㄊㄚ 是ㄕˋ shì shìh 我ㄨㄛˇ 的ㄉㄜ 好ㄏㄠˇ 朋ㄆㄥˊ 友ㄧㄡˇ 。

tā　shì　shéi　　　tā　shì　wǒ　de　hǎo　péng　yǒu
　　 shìh　　　　　　 shìh

Who is he?　　　He is my good friend.

② 課室活動：老師說：「請彎腰」，小朋友做彎腰動作。
老師如果只說：「彎腰」，小朋友不動。可延伸練習教室用語。

 連連看 **Match the right pictures**

1. 日

2. 木

3. 月

4. 山

5. 口

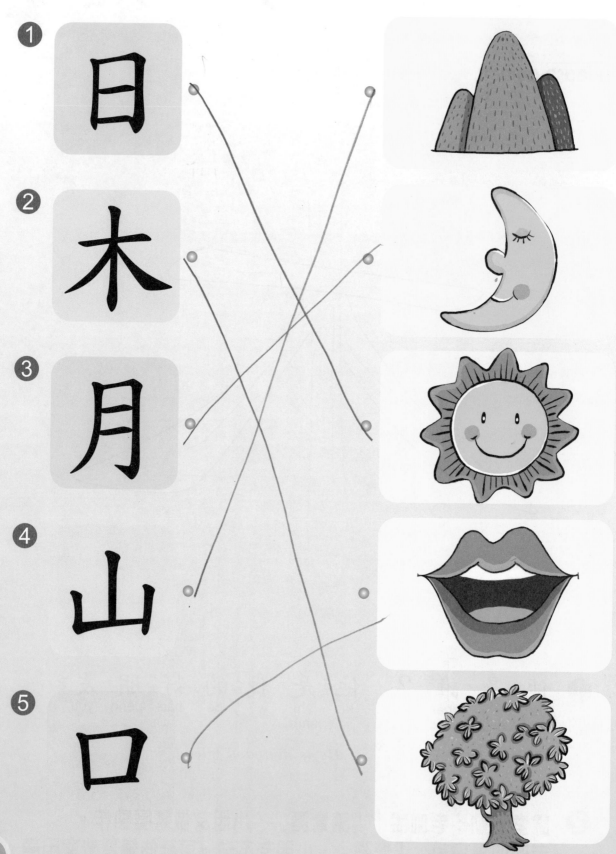

38

Tones	1st tone	2nd tone	3rd tone	4th tone
早	早			
山	山	山		
木	木			
十				
(牙)				

生活華語 第 K1 冊
Living Mandarin

海 外 指 導：費城頂好中文學校 Ding Hao Chinese School
紐西蘭華語文教學基金會
溫哥華台灣語言協會

輔　　　導：教育部

策 劃 者：生活華語教材委員會

創 作 編 寫：Betty FOO 張紀渝　　YU B. C. 余伯泉　　Alice JAO 饒淑惠
Whitney CHUANG 莊舒雯

編　　　輯：Alice JAO 饒淑惠　　Sonia CHANG 張雅容

美 編 印 刷：磊承印刷事業有限公司 www.lcprint.com.tw

彩 虹 筆 順：婁世美

繪　　　圖：鍾佳吟　　羅敏芬

音　　　樂：三雅錄音有限公司

教 學 指 引：www.skymandarin.org

出　　　版：社團法人台灣語言文化社

發　　　行：藍天華語有限公司　　Sky Mandarin Ltd.

發 行 部：(115)台北市南港區研究院路二段2巷28號
28, Lane 2, Academia Rd. Sec. 2, Taipei 115, Taiwan
TEL：886-2-2653-2717　　FAX：886-2-2653-2719
e-mail：skymandarin@gmail.com

版　　　次：2008年一版　　2010年二版
2011年三版